Ruth

The God Who Provides

Ru-NK-SS

**A Bible-Based Study
For Individuals and Groups
Complete with Leader's Guide**

**Lamplighters International
St. Louis Park, Minnesota, USA 55416
www.LamplightersUSA.org**

Fourth printing – June 2006

Lamplighters International
St. Louis Park, Minnesota USA 55416

Lamplighters International is a Christian discipleship ministry that publishes Bible-based, Christ-centered discipleship resources.

For additional information about the Lamplighters ministry resources contact: Lamplighters International 6301 Wayzata Blvd, St. Louis Park, Minnesota USA 55416 or visit our web site at www.LamplightersUSA.org.

ISBN # 1-931372-10-1
Order # – Ru-NK-SS

Contents

How to Use This Study

What is Lamplighters?

Lamplighters is a Christ-centered discipleship ministry that is designed to increase your understanding of God's Word and equip you to serve Him more effectively. Each Lamplighters Bible Study is a self-contained unit and an integral part of the entire discipleship ministry.

This study is comprised of five or ten individual lessons, depending on the format you choose. When you have completed the entire study you will have a much greater understanding of a significant portion of God's Word. You will also have learned several new truths that you can apply to your life.

How to Study a Lamplighters Lesson.

A Lamplighters study begins with prayer, your Bible, the weekly lesson, and a sincere desire to learn more about God's Word. The questions are presented in a progressive sequence as you work through the study material. You should not use Bible commentaries or other reference books until you have completed your weekly lesson and met with your weekly group. When you approach the Bible study in this way, you will have the opportunity to personally discover many valuable spiritual truths from the Word of God.

As you prepare for your lesson, find a quiet place to complete your weekly lesson. Each study (Part "a" or "b") will take approximately thirty minutes to complete. If you are new to Lamplighters materials, you should plan to spend more time on the first few lessons. Your weekly personal study time will decrease as you become familiar with the format. Soon you will look forward each week to discovering important life principles in the coming lessons.

You should write your answers in your own words in the space provided within the weekly studies. We have intentionally provided a significant amount of writing space for this purpose. Include appropriate verse references at the end of your carefully worded and thoughtful answers, unless the question calls for a personal opinion. The answers to the questions will be found in the Scripture references at the end of the questions or in the passages listed at the beginning of each study.

"*Do you think*" Questions

Each weekly study has a few "*do you think*" questions. These questions ask you to make personal applications from the Biblical truths you are learning. Make a special effort to answer these questions because they are designed to help you apply God's Word to your life. In the first two lessons the "*do you think*" questions are placed in italic print for easy identification. If you are part of a study group, your insightful answers to these questions could be a great source of spiritual encouragement to others.

The Lamplighters discipleship materials are designed for a variety of ministry applications. They have been used successfully in the following settings:

Self-study - Read the passage listed at the beginning of the weekly lesson. Seek to gain as much understanding from the Text as possible. Answer the questions in the space provided, using complete sentences if the space allows. Complete the entire lesson without looking at the Leader's Guide in the back of the book. Discipline yourself to answer all the questions so that you gain the maximum benefit from the lesson. When you have completed the lesson, read the corresponding portion of the Leader's Guide to gain greater understanding of the passage you have just studied.

One-on-one discipleship - Complete the entire lesson without referring to the Leader's Guide. If you are leading the one-on-one discipleship time meeting, become familiar with the Leader's Guide answers before you meet with the person you are discipling. Plan to meet for approximately one hour to discuss the lesson. If you are not the leader, do not look at the Leader's Guide until you have met for the meeting.

Small Group discipleship - The members of the discipleship group should complete their weekly lessons without referring to the Leader's Guide. The Group Leader should complete the lesson before he becomes thoroughly familiar with the Leader's Guide answers. A comprehensive ministry manual has been prepared for church leaders to help lead small groups effectively and implement the Lamplighters discipleship ministry into their church.

Class teaching (Adult or Senior High Sunday School Classes) - The pastor or teacher should complete the entire lesson before class, review the Leader's Guide answers, and prayerfully consider how to present the lesson. The class members should complete their weekly lessons in advance so that they can bring their thoughtful insights and questions to the class discussion time. The Teacher's Edition makes an excellent companion to this format and allows the teacher to design specific lessons appropriate in length and knowledge level for the students. For more information on combining these two products, contact Lamplighters or visit our website

Personal Questions

Occasionally you will be asked to respond to personal questions that you should do your best to answer. If you are part of a study group, you will not be asked to share any personal information about yourself. However, be sure to answer these questions for your own benefit because they will help you compare your present level of spiritual maturity to the Biblical principles presented in the lesson.

A Final Word

Throughout this study the masculine pronouns are often used in the generic sense to avoid awkward sentence construction. When the pronouns "he," "him," and "his" are used to refer to the Trinity (God the father, Jesus Christ and the Holy Spirit), they always refer to the masculine gender.

This Lamplighters study is presented after many hours of careful preparation. It is our prayer that it will help you **grow in the grace and knowledge of our Lord and Savior Jesus Christ. To Him be the glory both now and forever. Amen** (2 Pet. 3:18).

About the Author

John Alexander Stewart was born and raised near Winnipeg, Canada. He was drafted by the Pittsburgh Penguins (NHL) and played professional hockey for eight years. He was born again in 1977 when he accepted Jesus Christ alone for eternal life. He graduated from seminary in 1988. He served as a pastor for fifteen years. During this time he planted two Bible-believing churches. He also founded Lamplighters International and now serves as the executive director of the ministry.

Introduction

The Book of Ruth has been called the most beautiful short story ever written. It is a love story—not just about a man and a woman (Boaz and Ruth) or a daughter-in-law's love for her mother-in-law (Ruth and Naomi), but about God's unfailing love for all those who place their trust in Him. Ruth was a young Moabite widow who left her family and her homeland during a time of famine to care for her discouraged mother-in-law, Naomi. Ruth was seeking more than the sweet satisfaction that comes from unselfishly loving those in need. She was being drawn by the God of heaven who alone could satisfy the famine of her soul.

Historical Background

The first verse of Ruth (1:1) provides a valuable historical marker. **"Now it came to pass, in the days when the judges ruled"** refers to a definite period of Israelite history (1400-1050 BC), commonly known as Israel's "dark ages." This period of time was characterized by moral degradation, political corruption and spiritual blindness (cf. Ju. 2:10-23). A second historical marker in the Book of Ruth reveals that Ruth was the great-grandmother of King David (Ru. 4:17). David began his reign as king of Judah in 1010 BC. It is likely the events of the Book of Ruth occurred in the last half of the 12th century BC during the judgeship of Gideon. Many Biblical scholars believe that the events recorded in Ruth cover approximately ten to fifteen years (cf. Ruth 1:4; 4:13).

Purpose and Importance

There is no clear-cut, central theme of the Book of Ruth. The original purpose of Ruth may have been to provide a genealogical record of King David's right to the throne of Israel. Some scholars believe that the purpose of Ruth may be to show how God works behind the scenes to direct the affairs of human history (i.e., providence). A third purpose of the book may be to show that God's people can live godly lives even in the midst of social perversity. It is important to realize that the central figure of all Scripture is God, not man; and His Word is much more than an endless series of moral and ethical object lessons (e.g., Daniel loved God - follow his example; Jonah ran from God - don't follow his example.). Still others believe the main purpose is to reveal God's covenant faithfulness to individuals who honor Him regardless of the spiritual apathy of the community at large. Finally, some see Boaz, who rescued two impoverished women (Ruth and Naomi), as a prototype of the Great Redeemer, Jesus Christ, who came to rescue all mankind from spiritual destitution.

It is important to remember that the events in the Book of Ruth took place in the days when **"there was no king in Israel; everyone did what was right in his own eyes"** (Ju. 21:25). The book shines as a sunbeam of God's love during one of the darkest storms in Israel's history. God's vindication of Ruth's faithfulness has warmed the hearts of God's people and continues to give them courage to trust Him during their greatest trials.

The "Kinsman-Redeemer"

Perhaps the most difficult interpretive question in the Book of Ruth is the exact role assumed by Boaz as the kinsman-redeemer or close relative. The kinsman-redeemer (Hebrew *go'el*) of ancient Israel was responsible to protect the inheritance (i.e., property) of a deceased family member or members by marrying the relative's widow and raising up children in his name. The children resulting from this union would assume the name of the deceased and eventually inherit any property belonging to his family.

Study # 1a   *"Your God and My God"*

1. What has the Book of Ruth also been called? *The most beautiful short story ever written*

2. Give a brief biographical sketch of Ruth from the **Introduction** and from Ruth 1:2-5.
    born in Moab, married to Mahlon son of Naomi +

3. a. When did the events recorded in the Book of Ruth actually occur (v. 1; **Introduction***)?*

    b. What were the "**days when the judges ruled**" commonly known as in Israelite history?

4. a. Briefly describe the moral and spiritual conditions in Israel during the time of the Israelite judges (Ju. 2:10-23).

    b. Which famous Old Testament (hereafter, "OT") judge likely was governing during the events in the book of Ruth?

5. Approximately how many years do the events of the Book of Ruth span?

6. List the five possible purposes or central themes of the Book of Ruth.

7. Who or what is the central theme of all Scripture?

8. What was the role of the close relative or kinsman-redeemer of ancient Israel?

Study #1b   *"Your God and My God"*

9. Elimelech moved his family approximately fifty miles east of Bethlehem to the land of Moab (Ruth 1:1). Elimelech's decision, motivated by financial pressure, removed himself and his family from the Israelite community and the regular instruction of God's Word (i.e., the Law of Moses).

    a. List three things that happened to this man and his family during their time in Moab (Ru. 1:2-5).

    b. *Do you think* Elimelech's decision to move his family to Moab was wise? Why or why not?

10. A wise Christian husband will give serious consideration not only to where he moves his family, but also when he moves them (i.e., the spiritual condition of his family, the ages of his children, etc.). If a man removes himself and his family from the regular instruction of the truth and fellowship with God's people, what is an almost inevitable consequence (v. 4)?

11. Perhaps Elimelech justified the move to Moab by thinking that his stay would be temporary (Note: The Hebrew word for **dwell**, *"guwr,"* means to dwell or to reside as a stranger.)

    a. Describe a situation in your life that initially benefited you financially, but later had a negative spiritual effect on you and others (e.g., job transfer, taking a second job, a special project at home, etc.).

    b.   If you had the same opportunity again, what would you do differently?

12. A believer's desire to capitalize on a financial opportunity can blind his eyes to the spiritual dangers that lie ahead.

    a.   Give at least three negative consequences of desiring riches above all (1 Tim. 6:9-10).

    b.   The Christian is commanded to flee the love of money (1 Tim. 6:11). The word **"flee"** (Greek: *pleugo*-to flee, to escape safely by flight, to vanish) indicates that he must be in constant flight to escape this spiritual danger. What specific steps have you taken to flee the love of money

13. What spiritual counsel would you give a young Christian man who was seriously considering moving his family to an area that did not have a strong, Bible-believing church?

14. When Naomi heard that the Lord had visited His people by giving them food, she moved back to Israel (Ru. 1:6-7). Bible scholars define providence as God sustaining and governing the affairs of human destiny through secondary causation (i.e., nature, economics, etc.). Give at least one situation in your life when God's providence directed your life (e.g., a work layoff, a prolonged illness, a loved one's death, a family move as a child, etc.).

15. Naomi buried her husband and her two sons in Moab. Discouraged and destitute, she left Moab and her home to return to Judah (Ru. 1:7 ff.). Ruth and Orpah, her two widowed daughters-in-law, accompanied her as she began her journey.

   a. What two reasons did Naomi use in her attempt to persuade her daughters to return to Moab and its pagan practices (Ru. 1:11-15)?

   b. What other factor(s) *do you think* might have influenced Naomi's decision to encourage Ruth and Orpah to return to the land of Moab and its pagan influences (cf. Ru. 1:19-21)?

16. Ruth's decision to follow Naomi meant that she had to leave her home, her remaining family, and any financial inheritance her husband, Mahlon, might have acquired before his death. Ruth made a five-fold commitment to Naomi to convince her that she could not be persuaded to return to Moab. What were the five aspects of her commitment (Ru. 1:16-18)?

17. What is the most important spiritual truth taught in this lesson?

Psalm 119:105   *"Your word is a lamp to my feet and a light to my path."*

Study # 2a   *"Whose Young Woman Is This?"*

Read - Ruth 1:19-2:16; other references as given.

1. Ruth and Naomi made their way back to Bethlehem without noticeable difficulty (Ru. 1:19). How did the people of Bethlehem respond to their arrival (Ru. 1:19)?

2. Naomi, whose name means "sweetness" or "pleasant," told the women of Bethlehem to call her Mara (v. 20). List four things Naomi said about the Lord's treatment of her (Ru. 1:20-21).

3. Both Naomi and Ruth experienced great personal trials, but they responded to them in different ways. What differences do you notice between the way Naomi and Ruth responded to their difficulties?

4. Naomi's inability to see the Lord's provision led her to grumble about the Lord and testify against His goodness.

    a. Do you regularly grumble and complain when you experience trials?

b. What could you do differently to be a better witness for Christ during these times?

5. When Christians become embittered against God, they often lose the spiritual ability to see His good in their lives. List at least three ways God demonstrated His loving concern for Naomi even though she was unthankful (Ru. 1:6-22).

6. Bitterness is like a spiritual cancer, begining with an emotional wound from others failing to meet our expectations (Biblical or social). Unless a believer receives appropriate spiritual help, bitterness will grow in a person's life until it destroys him. What are some negative consequences that can occur when a believer secretly (and sometimes not so secretly) harbors resentment against God or another person (Heb. 12:15; Pro. 17:22)?

7. Why do you think some Christians become bitter against God even though they know He is good?

8. Ruth was a young widow living in a foreign land, far away from family and friends. The fact that there is no mention of any children from her marriage to Mahlon suggests that she might have been barren at the time (cf. Ru. 1:4-5). (Note: Barrenness in ancient times was a social stigma.) Apart from her hope in God, her future seemed to hold only the complaining companionship of her despondent mother-in-law, Naomi, and a life of poverty. Nevertheless, Ruth continued to exemplify virtue and emotional strength. What aspect of Ruth's character impresses you the most? Why?

9. An old Latin proverb says, "Providence assists not the idle." Since Ruth was a woman of action rather than reaction, she asked Naomi's permission to glean in the fields. Gleaning was a provision of the OT Law (cf. Lev. 19:9-10; 23:22; De. 24:19-22) that provided for the poor and needy of the land. Give three additional examples of God's providential care that these two women did not immediately recognize as such. (Ru. 2:3-5).

Study # 2b "Whose Young Woman Is This?"

Read - Ruth 1:19-2:16; other references as given.

10. The beginning of the beautiful romance that occurred between the older landowner Boaz and the younger widow Ruth began when he noticed her gleaning in his fields. Within this passage, there are several important principles about marital relationship development that God's people should adopt today.

    a. What is the first thing Boaz did after Ruth's presence caught his attention (Ru. 2:5-7)?

    b. What character qualities do you think Ruth manifested by her actions to glean in the fields that would make her an excellent wife (Ru. 2:3-9)?

11. Boaz spoke to Ruth for the first time without indicating that he had any relationship interest in her (Ru. 2:8 ff.).

    a. List three things Boaz said to Ruth that would have greatly comforted her (Ru. 2:8-9).

    b. How did Ruth respond to Boaz's attempt to meet her physical and emotional needs (Ru. 2:10)?

    c.   Why do you think it is so important for men and women who are attracted to each other to demonstrate this kind of concern for each other before they express any feelings of affection?

12. Boaz said to Ruth, "**It has been fully reported to me, all that you have done for your mother-in-law since the death of your husband**" (Ru. 2:11). In what way(s) do you think Boaz's knowledge of the death of her husband and her loyalty to Naomi would have been a special encouragement to Ruth?

13. A healthy relationship must begin with a genuine concern for the physical and emotional needs of the other person. What is the other important principle that should be established early in every new Christian relationship (Ru. 2:12; Pro. 3:6)?

14. When Ruth responded to Boaz's words of encouragement, she did something that every Christian wife would be wise to practice. What is it (Ru. 2:13)?

15. At mealtime Boaz asked Ruth to eat with the reapers and himself (Ru. 2:14).

   a. What did Boaz do during this time that demonstrated mature spiritual conduct (Ru. 2:14)?

   b. What specific things could a Christian do to honor his spouse in public?

16. After the meal, Boaz told his servants to leave some extra grain for Ruth without letting her know what they were doing (Ru. 2:15-16).

   a. Boaz's leaving the grain for Ruth, rather than just giving it to her, revealed that he understood what important spiritual truth (Ru. 2:15-16; Pro. 31:31)?

   b. In what way(s) do you think Boaz's carefully devised plan accomplished a greater objective than simply providing Ruth with a generous supply of grain?

Psalm 119:105 "Your word is a lamp to my feet and a light to my path."

Study # 3a   **A Woman of Virtue**

Read - Ruth 3:1-18; other references as given.

1. Beginning in chapter three, the story of Ruth enters a new phase. Even a casual reading of the text reveals that Naomi's attitude toward life had changed significantly since their initial return to Bethlehem (Ru. 1:13, 20-22; 3:1-4). Why was Naomi now more hopeful (Ru. 3:1-2)?

2. Naomi, wise in the customs of her homeland, recognized an opportunity that might rescue Ruth and herself from a life of abject poverty and social obscurity. She became a matchmaker, hoping to arrange a marriage between Ruth and Boaz.

    a. What plan did Naomi recommend to Ruth (Ru. 3:1-4)?

    b. What did Ruth say in response to Naomi's plan (v. 5)?

3. It is easy for Christians to regard Ruth's response to Naomi as being one of faith and loyal obedience because we know the story of her life. On the other hand, it would also be understandable to view Ruth's willingness to follow Naomi's plan as foolish innocence or naïveté. What do you think is the difference between the kind of faith that leads Christians to a warranted trust in others and the kind of faith that is dangerously foolish?

4. Perhaps Naomi's recommendation that Ruth go to the threshing floor in the dark seemed strange or even dangerous to Ruth (cf. Ru. 2:22). Why do you think Ruth responded so positively to Naomi's plan (vv. 1-4)?

5. a. Describe a situation in your life when you received advice from another person (parent, employer, pastor, etc.) that seemed unrealistic or even wrong at the time, but you later realized that it was wise counsel.

    b. What did you learn from this experience?

6. It is likely that Naomi felt she needed to act as a matchmaker because neither Boaz nor Ruth could conceive that the other might be agreeable to such an idea. While Naomi's role as matchmaker is not dissimilar to the modern practice of arranging a date for two people, the Bible does record a few instances when marriages were arranged by a third party (cf. Gen. 21:21; 24:1-8; 38:6).

    a. Now that America has the highest divorce rate in the world, many Christians and marriage counselors are beginning to reevaluate the American approach to marital relationships (i.e., dating, engagement). What problems, if any, do you see with this modern approach of choosing a lifetime marriage partner?

    b. What Biblical advice would you give a young Christian who wanted to be sure to marry the right individual?

7. One commentator says, *"... the book of Ruth is much more than the record of the marriage of a rejected alien to a respected Jew. It is a picture of how we come to the Great Kinsman-Redeemer, Jesus Christ, in salvation as we rescue our impoverished souls from spiritual famine. We must cleanse ourselves and put on our royal garments in preparation to meeting Him. He, like Boaz, will tell us what to do."* Do you agree with the interpretation? Why or why not?

8. The threshing floor upon which Boaz winnowed his grain was an elevated level area used for this purpose by the inhabitants of Bethlehem. (Note: The word *Bethlehem* means *house of bread;* a name derived from the bountiful harvests that came from the valleys to the east and south.) When it was Boaz's turn to use the threshing floor, he winnowed the grain late into the evening to take advantage of the evening breeze (cf. Ru. 3:2) and then slept nearby to protect his harvest from theft (Ru. 3:7). In the middle of the night, Boaz discovered someone at his feet (Ru. 3:8). What two responses did Ruth give when Boaz's inquired about her identity (Ru. 3:9)?

9. No doubt Ruth was somewhat apprehensive about Boaz's reaction to her proposal. List three things Boaz said that would have greatly comforted Ruth (Ru. 3:10-11).

Study # 3b   A Woman of Virtue

Read - Ruth 3:1-18; other references as given.

10. What had Ruth not done, the absense of which act contributed to her reputation as a virtuous woman?

11. Boaz called Ruth **a virtuous woman** (Ru. 3:11). He based his comment on his own assessment of her character and the reputation that she had gained among the people of Bethlehem. The Bible instructs God's people to encourage one another by offering them sincere praise. On the other hand, the Scriptures denounce flattery, condemning it as deceit and hatred (Job 17:5; Pro. 6:24; 29:5). What do you think is the difference between flattery (a sin) and sincere praise for others?

12. Ruth asked Boaz to assume the role of her kinsman-redeemer. Boaz was probably surprised but evidently pleased with the opportunity to marry this woman of virtue. What problem arose that complicated his unconditional acceptance of her offer (Ru. 3:12)?

13. Shortly before the first light of morning Ruth and Boaz arose (Ru. 3:14). He gave her six measures of barley. Why didn't he wait until daylight to perform this task?

14. Many young, unmarried couples fail to realize that their blossoming new relationship affects more than themselves. Someone once said, "You don't marry an individual, you marry a family." While this is only partially true, a wise, Christian couple will seriously consider the effects their relationship has on other family members.

    a. How did Ruth demonstrate sensitivity to Naomi's emotional needs at this time (Ru. 3:16)?

    b. How did Boaz attempt to meet Naomi's emotional needs during this time?

15. What specific things do you regularly do to assure your extended family members (parents, in-laws, etc.) of your continued love and devotion?

16. In addition to the things you mentioned in your answer to question #15, what additional things could you do to assure extended family members of your concern for their welfare without violating your relationship with your spouse? (Note: Husbands and wives could consider discussing this with each other or as a family.)

Psalm 119:105 "Your word is a lamp to my feet and a light to my path."

Study # 4a The Fruit of Faithfulness

Read - Ruth 4:1-22; other references as given.

1. Naomi was correct when she told Ruth that Boaz would settle the matter about the kinsman-redeemer as soon as possible (cf. Ru. 3:18). It was probably very early the next morning when Boaz went to the city gate (the place where official public business was conducted) in anticipation of finding the close relative of whom he had spoken (Ru. 4:1). What two things did Boaz do when he found the relative who was qualified to be the kinsman-redeemer (Ru. 4:1-2)?

2. Boaz presented the facts of the case clearly, hoping that the man would decide not to redeem the property. What was the close relative's initial response when Boaz told him that Naomi wanted to sell the land belonging to her deceased husband Elimelech (Ru. 4:3-4)?

3. Why do you think Boaz said he would become the kinsman-redeemer if the close relative decided not to redeem the property (Ru. 4:4)?

4. a. What additional information did Boaz provide the close relative that caused him to change his mind about the intended purchase (Ru. 4:5)?

    b. Why did the close relative change his mind about buying the land after learning his decision would mean acquiring Ruth as well?

5.   Although Boaz had a strong desire to marry Ruth, he gave the unnamed kinsman-redeemer every opportunity to redeem the land and acquire Naomi and Ruth (Ru. 4:4). In what way(s) do you think Boaz's approach to the situation would have affected his future marital relationship to Ruth?

6.   It is easy for God's people to say they have peace about a particular decision, but impossible to experience that peace without totally yielding themselves to God's will. How can a Christian differentiate between God's will and simply fleshly desires in the midst of making decisions?

7.   Boaz asked ten Bethlehem elders (Hebrew *zaqan* - to have a beard) to serve in an official capacity as he attempted to settle this issue. During times of dispute, the elders would sit and listen as opposing parties presented their cases. They would weigh the evidence and render their official decision on the matter. What other responsibility did the elders fulfill in this situation (Ru. 4:9-11)?

8. The transaction was sealed with the transfer of a sandal (Ru. 4:7) (Note: The Hebrew is not clear whose sandal was transferred, but most scholars believe Boaz received the sandal as evidence of the transaction.) What did Boaz say in the presence of the elders that obliged him to be the official kinsman-redeemer of Elimelech's family (Ru. 4:10)?

9. The ten elders of Bethlehem and all the other people at the city gate pronounced a threefold blessing on Boaz for his willingness to become the kinsman-redeemer. What three things did they hope would happen (Ru. 4:11)?

10. In the days when there was no king in Israel and "**everyone did what was right in his own eyes**" (Ju. 21:25, Ru. 1:1), God raised up a young Gentile widow named Ruth to show that God continues to honor those who honor Him. Give two additional examples of God's willingness to honor Ruth for her faith in Him (Ru. 4:13).

Study # 4b   The Fruit of Faithfulness

11. The women of Bethlehem said, "**Blessed be the Lord who has not left you this day without a close relative, and may his name be famous in Israel!**" (Ru. 4:14). Does the phrase **close relative** (Heb. *go'el*) refer to Boaz or to the son born to Ruth and Boaz (Ru. 4:14-15)?

12. Boaz had previously called Ruth a woman of virtuous conduct and self-restraint (cf. Ru. 3:11). Now Ruth receives an endorsement from her peers - the women of the city. What did they say about her (Ru. 4:15)?

13. Neighbor women named the child Obed (Heb. *servant;* cf. Obadiah - servant of Yahweh). They said, "**There is a son born to Naomi!**"(Ru. 4:17). Why do you think they would make this statement when the child was actually born to Boaz and Ruth?

14. God vindicated the faith of a young widow who dared to trust in Him. God honored the faith of an older single man who waited patiently for God's choice of a lifetime mate. God patiently ministered to an older woman who lost a husband, her two sons, and her confidence in His sovereign goodness.

    a.   What character qualities do you most appreciate about Boaz? Why?

    b.   What character qualities do you most admire about Ruth? Why?

15. Name the most significant spiritual truths taught in the Book of Ruth?

Congratulations: You have just finished a brief but challenging study of Ruth. The Book of Ruth is more than a beautiful story of a young Gentile widow who finds a husband and a home - it is the revelation of God and the unfolding of His sovereign plan as He works providentially to honor those who honor Him. Ruth was a woman who chose to love God, and that decision led her to the community of God's people and the comfort of His love, "An inheritance incorruptible and undefiled and that does not fade away" (1 Peter 1:4).

May God help us to trust Him so that we too might experience the presence of His love and the provision of His grace. Amen.

Study # 1   *"Your God and My God"*

1.   The most beautiful short story ever written.

2.   Ruth was a young Gentile (Moabite) widow who left her family and homeland to care for her mother-in-law Naomi.

3.   a.   The events of the Book of Ruth occurred during the days when Israel was governed by the judges (Ru. 1:1; ca. 1400-1050 BC).
      b.   Israel's "dark ages."

4.   a.   The Israelites regularly forsook the Lord and worshipped the pagan idols of the nations around them (Ju. 2:12). Although the people did repent on a few occasions, they always returned to their evil ways. The Lord sent judges to rule over them, but once the judges died, they returned to their sinful ways (Ju. 2:19). God allowed hostile neighboring nations to oppress the people of Israel so that they would turn back to Him (Ju. 2:20-23).
      b.   Gideon.

5.   Ten to fifteen years.

6.   1.   The original purpose of Ruth may have been to provide a genealogical record of King David's right to the throne of Israel.
      2.   Ruth may have been written to show how God works behind the scenes to direct the affairs of human history (i.e., providence).
      3.   A third purpose of the book may be to show that God's people can live godly lives despite social perversity.
      4.   The main purpose may be to reveal God's covenant faithfulness to individuals who honor Him regardless of the spiritual apathy of the community at large.
      5.   A fifth purpose some scholars believe is the central theme of Ruth is to show Boaz as a prototype of the Great Redeemer, Jesus Christ.

7.   God.

8.   The close relative or kinsman-redeemer (Heb. *go'el*) of ancient Israel was a male relative of a deceased family member who assumed the responsibility of protecting the estate (property) of the deceased by marrying the relative's widow and raising up children in his name. The children from the union of the kinsman-redeemer and the widow eventually inherited all property belonging to the estate of the father.

9. a.   1. Elimelech died (v. 3). 2. Elimelech's two sons, Mahlon and Chilion, married Moabite women (v. 4). 3. Mahlon and Chilion died (v. 5). 4. Naomi was left stranded in a foreign land.

      b.   Although nothing in the immediate passage specifically denounces Elimelech's move to Moab, the paganized nation of Moab had a negative effect on his family. Neither his death nor his sons' deaths should be construed as an act of divine judgment, yet his willingness to remove his family from the worship of God and regular fellowship with God's people appears to be unwise because it placed his grown sons in a pagan environment that resulted in their marriage to Gentile women. God gave the sons of Israel the Promised Land and promised to provide for their needs within the land if they obeyed Him. Elimelech's move to Moab removed his family from the instruction of the law of Moses and the support of those few who continued to be faithful to God throughout the period of the judges. While God's people are often tempted to "take matters into their own hands" during a time of testing, their first responsibility should be to examine their own relationship to God and make sure that their intended plans do not violate any direct commands of Scripture. They should also try to evaluate whether their plans will have any negative long-term spiritual consequences on themselves and others.

10. His children will often marry non-believers.

11. a.   Answers will vary.

      b.   Answers will vary.

12. a.   1.   They easily fall into temptation (v. 9).
           2.   They often find themselves ensnared or trapped as a result of their overspending and an inability to control their financial lusts (v. 9).
           3.   If they do not realize their sin and repent, this entrapment often will bring them to ruination (v. 9). This ruination could refer to the destruction of their families and their lives, both emotionally and physically.

      b.   Answers will vary but should include the following:
           1.   The believer should consciously set his mind on eternal values.
           2.   The believer should practice a habit of regular financial giving through a local, Bible-believing church.
           3.   The believer should be careful to live within the financial means that God has given him.
           4.   The believer should practice regular sacrificial giving to the needs of others. Other answers could apply.

13. The Christian man should be counseled to see the potential long-term spiritual effects on his wife and children. He should be lovingly exhorted to examine his priorities in relation to eternity. He should be encouraged to seek the counsel of several godly believers so that he might receive the wisdom of their spiritual understanding (cf. Pro. 11:14).

14. Answers will vary.

15. a. 1. Naomi told Ruth and Orpah that she had no way to provide for their needs (vv. 11-14).
    2. Naomi told Ruth that Orpah had decided to go back and that Ruth should follow her sister-in-law.
    b. 1. Naomi had not lost sight of God's sovereign authority over all nations (cf. Ru. 1:6, 8, 9), but she had become so discouraged that she had lost sight of the power of the Lord to provide for her needs.
    2. Naomi could not see the plan God had in store for both Ruth and herself and possibly even Orpah.
    3. She had become bitter in her spirit against God and her attitude negatively affected her ability to minister to others.
    4. She could have been embarrassed that her sons had married Gentile women.
    5. She allowed the trials of life to preoccupy her thinking, distort her perspective and hinder her witness. Other answers could apply.

16. 1. Ruth said she would not abandon Naomi (**"wherever you go, I will go"** [v. 16]).
    2. Ruth said she would help provide for her daily needs (**"wherever you lodge, I will lodge"** [v. 16]).
    3. Ruth said she would become fully integrated into the Israelite community (**"Your people shall be my people"** [v. 16]).
    4. Ruth said she would worship the one true God (**"your God, my God"** [v. 16]).
    5. Ruth said she would be loyal to Naomi until death (**"Where you die, I will die"** [v. 17]).

17. Answers will vary.

Study # 2   *"Whose Young Woman Is This?"*

1.   The people of Bethlehem were surprised to hear about Naomi's return, and the women of the city wondered if she was really the Naomi. Apparently Naomi's stay in Moab had a considerable aging effect upon her.

2.
   1. She said the Almighty had dealt very bitterly with her (v. 20).
   2. She said the Lord brought her back to Bethlehem empty (v. 21).
   3. She said the Lord testified against her (v. 21).
   4. She said the Almighty had afflicted her (v. 21).

3.   Naomi blamed God for her problems and complained to others about the way the Lord had treated her. According to the text, Ruth did not utter a single complaint about her problems despite her own the loss of a husband and stress of moving to a foreign land. Ruth also had the burden of caring for her despondent mother-in-law Naomi who complained about how the Lord had treated her. It appears that Ruth chose to make the best of a bad situation without compounding the problem with complaints to others.

4.
   a. Answers will vary.
   b. Answers will vary depending on the answer given in part "a."

5.
   1. The Lord caused the famine to cease in Israel at the time of Naomi's greatest need (v. 6).
   2. The Lord allowed Naomi to hear a report of the famine being over in Israel (v. 6).
   3. The Lord directed Ruth's heart to follow Naomi back to Israel (vv. 15-18).
   4. The Lord protected Naomi and Ruth during the perilous journey back to Bethlehem (v. 19).
   5. The Lord directed them to return at the beginning of the barley harvest (v. 22).

6.
   1. Bitterness leads to a variety of troubles (Heb. 12:15).
   2. Resentment and bitterness can be infectious as one person passes his feelings of ill will onto another (Heb. 12:15).
   3. Bitterness and resentment can cause the person's health to suffer (Pro. 17:22, **"dries up the bones"**).

7.
   1. They are selfish and resent God for not allowing things to go their way.
   2. They forget that God has a higher purpose for their lives than their perpetual happiness and ease of living.
   3. They have allowed themselves to focus on earthly things and they become jealous of others and resentful against God for not providing them with material things.

4. They believe that God had somehow failed them then resented His unwillingness to bless them in spite of their bitterness. Other answers could apply.

8. Answers will vary.

9. 1. Ruth went to glean in the field of Boaz, a relative of Elimelech (v. 3).
   2. Boaz came from Bethlehem and "happened" to arrive where Ruth was working on that particular day (v. 4).
   3. Boaz noticed Ruth as she gleaned in his field (v. 5).

10. a. Boaz asked his servant about Ruth's identity.
    b. 1. Humility. Gleaning in the fields was a menial task. 2. Diligence. Gleaning was hard work, requiring a great deal of effort for a meager return. 3. Courage. Ruth gleaned among workers who might physically attack her (cf. Ru. 2:9). 4. Initiative. Ruth did not wait for God to miraculously provide food for her and Naomi. Other answers could apply.

11. a. 1. Boaz told Ruth that she could continue to glean in his field (v. 8).
       2. Boaz told his servants not to harm Ruth (v. 9).
       3. Boaz told Ruth to drink from the water jars if she got thirsty.
    b. Ruth fell on her face, bowed to the ground and thanked Boaz for his generosity. She said that his kindness was especially appreciated since she was a foreigner.
    c. The mutual demonstration of genuine concern for members of the opposite sex is important because it establishes the priority of pure, Biblical love. Both parties experience a growing confidence that the actions of each other are not simply motivated by physical attraction or selfish pursuit. When the priority of mutual concern and growing sacrificial love is established early in the relationship, it fortifies a future marriage against the threats of disunity.

12. 1. Boaz's statement would have served as an unofficial welcome to the Israelite community, reassuring Ruth that she would not be totally rejected as a foreigner.
    2. Boaz's statement would have helped Ruth realize that others appreciated her ministry to her despondent mother-in-law, Naomi, who was not particularly grateful for anything at this time.
    3. Boaz's statement would have served as an endorsement of Ruth's willingness to serve her mother-in-law, fortifying her against the other's comments and her own natural self-doubts.
    4. Boaz's statement about the death of Ruth's husband might have served as a note of sympathetic understanding, helping ease the pain of her husband's death. (Note: It is impossible to tell from the text (cf. Ru. 1:4) whether Elimelech's family lived a total of ten years in Moab or if they lived there ten years after Mahlon's and Chilion's marriage.) Other answers could apply.

13. Christians should establish the presence of God in their conversations with others by testifying of His goodness and His willingness to reward those who trust in Him.

14. Ruth expressed sincere appreciation for Boaz's acts of kindness. Ruth's stated her praise in simple expressions of gratitude that assured Boaz that she noticed his kindness and appreciated his sensitivity toward her.

15. a. Boaz had Ruth sit beside the reapers, and he served her in the presence of his other servants. By doing so, he honored her in the presence of his closest associates. There can be little doubt that Ruth's satisfaction (v. 14) extended far beyond her physical appetite.

    b. Answers will vary.

16. a. Boaz recognized the basic need of all people to experience a sense of personal accomplishment. God's original command, **"Be fruitful and multiply, and fill the earth, and subdue it; and have dominion over the fish of the sea"** (Gen. 1:28) was given both to man and woman. A husband acts wisely when he realizes that his wife seeks accomplishment as much as he does.

    b. Ruth received the satisfaction that God was blessing her meager effort to provide for herself and Naomi. Ruth had taken a huge step of faith when she committed to care for Naomi, and her new cache of grain was evidence of God's endorsement of her commitment. The sense of accomplishment and blessing Ruth received as a result of Boaz's wise action strengthened her faith and lifted her spirits.

Study # 3   A Woman of Virtue

1. Naomi thought that Boaz might be willing to fulfill the role of kinsman-redeemer for Ruth and herself. If Boaz would be willing to assume this role, both Ruth and Naomi would be rescued from their present dilemma. It is also possible that Naomi was beginning to recognize that the Lord was honoring Ruth's willingness to live by faith.

2. a. Naomi told Ruth to wash and anoint herself, put on her best clothes, and go down to the threshing floor where Boaz was winnowing his grain (v. 3). She was to notice where Boaz had chosen to sleep for the night without letting him know that she had noticed. After dark, Ruth was to go to the place where he was sleeping, uncover his feet, and cover herself with the garment. Boaz would then notice her and tell her what next to do (v. 4).

    b.   **"All that you say to me I will do."**

3.   1.   The individual who exhibits Biblical faith continues to place his confidence in God, but the individual who exercises blind faith continually places his faith in people.

      2.   The individual who lives by Biblical faith considers Scriptural principles, prohibitions and promises to govern decisions, but the naïve individual allows others to think for himself.

      3.   The individual who lives by Biblical faith recognizes that he has a continuing responsibility to God for his decisions. On the other hand, the naïve individual, who blindly follows another person, often believes that he is absolved of any personal responsibility before God. He believes that God will not hold him responsible for his actions because he is simply trusting the decisions of another person. Other answers could apply.

4.   1.   Naomi stated the reason for her plan (**"shall I not seek security for you"**). This would assure Ruth that Naomi's plan was not born out of bitterness.

      2.   Naomi offered Ruth a detailed plan (vv. 2-4). This would have reassured Ruth that Naomi had given careful consideration to the various aspects of her idea.

5.   a.   Answers will vary.

    b.   Answers will vary.

6.   a.   1.   The modern approach to dating often leads to premature emotional bonding which inhibits a person's ability to objectively assess the other person's character. It is difficult for an emotionally-bonded individual to make an accurate assessment of the other person because he often sees the other person's desirable qualities but is blinded to his faults. Many people will say after marriage, "I never saw these negative habits in my spouse before we were married."

        2.   The modern dating approach, with its preoccupation with physical attraction, discourages the normal development of the friendship factor, an essential ingredient of a good marriage. Other answers could apply.

    b.   1.   A young Christian man (or woman) should develop his own personal relationship with God. This will help him develop spiritual discernment needed to choose a good marriage partner.

2.   He should attempt to be content in his present state of singleness, realizing that God has ordained it for him at the time. He should become involved in Christian service through a Bible-believing church, using his time and talents to serve the Lord. Individuals who are anxious to be married often compromise God's best for their lives.

3.   He should continue to pray for God's leading for every area of his life, including marriage.

4.   He should realize that marriage is a lifelong commitment, which must be approached with a great degree of gravity.

5.   He should make a personal commitment not to date an unsaved person.

6.   He should attempt to allow a relationship to develop carefully through the normal stages of acquaintance, friendship, companionship, and lifelong commitment, being careful not to allow himself to become emotionally attached until he is prepared to make a lifelong commitment to the other person.

7.   No.

1.   The Christian does not rescue himself from his spiritual poverty prior to salvation – Christ alone can save (cf. Acts 4:12; Jn. 14:6; Eph. 2:8-9).

2.   The believer does not cleanse himself in preparation for meeting Christ - Christ cleanses him by the washing of regeneration (cf. Ti. 3:5-6).

3.   The believer does not put on his royal garments in preparation for meeting Christ; rather he is clothed by God (2 Cor. 5:2-4). The quotation given in this question is a good example of what conservative Bible scholars call an "allegorical method" of interpretation, which is a subjective way of trying to understand God's Word that regularly leads to unwarranted speculations of the meaning of a passage and causes the student to miss the main point of the passage. When a student adopts an allegorical interpretation of the Bible, his imagination, rather than the Bible itself, becomes the epicenter of all truth. (Note: The thought that the close relative or kinsman-redeemer Boaz is a prototype of Christ is not supported by any Biblical references.)

8.   1.   Ruth said she was his maid.

2.   Ruth asked Boaz to take his maidservant under his wing (i.e., to assume the role of the kinsman-redeemer).

9.   1.   Boaz said that he recognized Ruth's actions as honorable (**"you have shown more kindness at the end than at the beginning"** [v. 10]).

2.   Boaz told her not to worry because he would do what she was asking (v. 11).

3.   Boaz praised Ruth by calling her **"a virtuous woman"** (v. 11).

10. Ruth had not run after the younger Israelite men to get married.

11. 1. Genuine praise of others builds them up in the faith. Flattery is an attempt to build ourselves up by mentally manipulating others for our benefit.
    2. Genuine praise is a virtue commended by Scripture, but flattery is a sin condemned by God.
    3. Genuine praise glorifies God, but flattery glorifies man (i.e., the one who is doing the flattering).
    4. Genuine praise promotes unity among people as it seeks to build others up, but flattery promotes disunity because it leads to suspicion and mistrust when the recipients of that flattery realize the insincerity.

12. Although Boaz was willing to become Ruth's kinsman-redeemer, another relative had the first right of refusal.

13. Boaz wanted to protect Ruth's reputation by avoiding any hint of suspicion regarding her stay with him during the night.

14. a. When Ruth returned to Naomi in the morning, she told her **"all that the man had done for her."**
    b. Boaz gave Ruth six measures of grain and told Ruth that he did not want her to go back to her mother-in-law empty-handed (v. 17). Ruth faithfully conveyed Boaz's words to Naomi.

15. Answers will vary.

16. 1. Reassure them of your commitment to meet their physical needs when they can't provide for themselves.
    2. Reassure them of your physical help when their health prevents them from doing things they need to do.
    3. Reassure them of your love and appreciation for their care throughout your childhood and adult years.
    4. Reassure them of God's continuing willingness to use them in His service. Other answers could apply.

Study # 4   The Fruit of Faithfulness

1. 1. Boaz asked the man to sit down for a while to discuss the matter.
   2. He asked ten of the elders of the city to join them as witnesses to his discussion with the close relative.

2. The close relative said he would redeem the property.

3. 1. Boaz wanted to marry Ruth.

2. Boaz probably offered to redeem the property if the other man did not do so. By doing this, Boaz released the man from his social obligation to the family. (Note: The Law of Moses taught that the man who rejected an opportunity to fulfill the role of kinsman-redeemer should face social repercussions for his unwillingness to assist the family in their time of need [cf. Dt. 25:5-10].)

4. a. Boaz told the man that, if he purchased Elimelech's land, he would have to acquire Ruth as his wife also.
   b. The close relative was afraid that marrying Ruth might jeopardize his own inheritance.

5. Boaz's approach to the negotiations that transpired between the close relative and himself would have given him confidence that his marriage to Ruth was God's will for their lives. When believers trust God by not attempting to manipulate life affairs, they experience the peace of God that assures them God directed their steps.

6. 1. The Christian should continue to dedicate himself to God as a living sacrifice. God has promised to direct the believer's life and give him the assurance that his actions are in accordance with the plan of God (cf. Pro. 3:6). Just as Boaz placed the situation totally in the hands of the Lord, believers should also trust God to direct their lives.
   2. The Christian should examine his own plans and heart motives, determining if they will glorify God or self.
   3. The believer should seek competent Christian counsel from others if he is unable to determine the source of his problem or if he is plagued by lingering doubts.

7. They served as witnesses of the negotiations that transpired between the close relative and Boaz.

8. Boaz stated in the presence of the witnesses that he had acquired Ruth the Moabitess to be his wife in order to raise up the name of the deceased. This statement meant that Boaz recognized that the firstborn male child (in this case Obed) would become the rightful heir of any property he was purchasing from the estate of Elimelech.

9. 1. They hoped that Ruth would bear Boaz many children.
   2. They hoped that the Lord would bless him financially.
   3. They hoped that he would become famous in Bethlehem.

10. 1. The Lord enabled Ruth to conceive and gave her a child (v. 13).
    2. The Lord gave her a son who would be able to redeem the property and restore the family name when he grew up.

11. The child Obed (v. 15).

12. The women said that Ruth loved Naomi and that she was better than seven sons. (Note: The number seven symbolizes completion.) The tribute is striking considering the importance placed on sons in the OT. The women of Bethlehem were giving Ruth the ultimate compliment.

13. Many scholars believe that this statement is more than an acknowledgment of the grandmother-grandson relationship that existed between Naomi and Obed. They believe that this was official recognition of Naomi's adoption of Obed as her son and the future legal heir to her deceased husband's property. Obed would be Boaz's biological son but he would also be the legal son and heir to Elimelech's property. He would also be Ruth's biological son and Naomi's and Ruth's kinsman-redeemer.

14. a. Answers will vary.
    b. Answers will vary.

15. Answers will vary.

The Final Exam

Every person will eventually stand before God in judgment – The Final Exam.

The Bible says, *"And as it is appointed for men to die once, but after this the judgment" (Hebrews 9:27).*

May I ask you a question? *"If you died today, do you know for certain that you would go to heaven?"* I do not ask you if you are religious or if you are a church member; nor do I ask if you have had some encounter with God—a meaningful, spiritual experience. I do not even ask you if you believe in God or angels, or if you are trying to live a good life. The question I am asking you is this: *"If you died today, do you know for certain that you would go to heaven?"*

When you die, you will stand alone before God in judgment. You will either be saved for all eternity or you will be separated from God for all eternity in what the Bible calls the lake of fire (Romans 14:12; Revelations 20:11-15). Tragically, many religious people who believe in God are not going to be accepted by Him when they die.

> *"Many will say to Me in that day, `Lord, Lord, have we not prophesied in Your name, cast out demons in Your name, and done many wonders in Your name?' And then I will declare to them, `I never knew you. Depart from Me, you who practice lawlessness!'" (Matthew 7:22-23)*

God loves you and wants you to go to heaven (John 3:16; 2 Peter 3:9). If you are not sure where you will spend eternity, you are not prepared to meet God. God wants you to know for certain that you will go to heaven.

> *"Behold, now is the accepted time; behold, now is the day of salvation. (2 Corinthians 6:2).*

The words **"behold"** and **"now"** are repeated because God wants you to know that you can be saved today. You do not need to hear those terrible words, *"Depart from Me..."!*

Jesus Himself said, *"You must be born again"* (John 3:7). These are not the words of a pastor, a church or a particular denomination; they are the words of Jesus Christ Himself. You <u>must</u> be born again (saved from eternal damnation) before you die; otherwise, it will be too late when you die! You can know for certain today that God will accept you into heaven when you die.

> *"These things I have written to you who believe in the name of the Son of God, that you may <u>know</u> that you have eternal life ..." (1 John 5:13)*

The phrase, *" you may know"* means that you can know for certain before you die that you will go to heaven. To be born again, you must understand and believe (this means to place your faith in) four essential spiritual truths. These truths are trustworthy, right from the Bible, not some man-made religious traditions.

Now let's consider these four essential spiritual truths:

1St Essential Spiritual Truth. <u>**The Bible teaches that you are a sinner and separated from God.**</u>

No one is righteous in God's eyes, including you. To be righteous means to be totally without sin, even a single act.

> *"There is none righteous, no, not one; There is none who understands; There is none who seeks after God. They have all turned aside; They have together become unprofitable; There is none who does good, no, not even one." (Romans 3:10-12).*

> *"For all have sinned and fall short of the glory of God" (Romans 3:23).*

Look at the words God uses to show that all men are sinners – **none, not one, all turned aside, not even one.** God is making a point – all men are sinners, including you. No man is good (perfectly without sin) in His sight. The reason is sin.

Have you ever lied, lusted, hated someone, stolen anything or taken God's name in vain, even once? These are sins. One sin makes you a sinner and unrighteous in God's eyes.

Are you willing to admit to God that you are a sinner? If you are, then tell Him right now you have sinned. You can say the words in your heart or out loud; it doesn't matter. But be honest with God. Check the box if you admit you are a sinner.

> ❑ *God, I admit I am a sinner in your eyes.*

2nd Essential Spiritual Truth. <u>**The Bible teaches that you cannot save yourself.**</u>

Man's sin is a very serious problem in the eyes of God. Your sin separates you from God, both now and for all eternity unless you are born again.

> *"For the wages of sin is death ..." (Romans 6:23).*

> *"And you He made alive, who were dead in trespasses and sins" (Ephesians 2:1).*

Wages are payments a person earns for what he or she has done. Your sin has earned you the wages of death, which means separation from God. If you die without ever having been born again, you will be separated from God after death.

You cannot save yourself or purchase your entrance into heaven. The Bible says that man is, *"... not redeemed with corruptible things, like gold or silver ..."* (1 Peter 1:18). If you owned all the money in the world, you could not buy your entrance into heaven nor can you buy your way into heaven with good works.

> *"For by grace you are saved through faith, and that <u>not of yourselves</u>, it is the gift of God, <u>not of works lest any man should boast</u>"* (Ephesians 2:8-9).

The Bible says salvation is, *"not of yourselves"*, *"... not of works, lest anyone should boast."* Salvation from eternal judgment cannot be earned by doing good works – it is a gift of God. There is nothing you can do to purchase your way into heaven because you are already unrighteous in God's eyes.

If you understand you cannot save yourself, then tell God right now that you are a sinner, separated from Him and you cannot save yourself. Check the box below if you have just done that.

❏ *God, I admit that I am separated from You because of my sin. I realize that I cannot save myself.*

Now let's look at the third essential spiritual truth.

3rd Essential Spiritual Truth. <u>The Bible teaches that Jesus Christ died on the cross to pay the complete penalty for your sin and to purchase a place in heaven for you.</u>

Jesus Christ, the sinless Son of God, lived a perfect life, died on the cross and rose from the dead to pay the penalty for your sin and purchase a place in heaven for you. He died on the cross on your behalf, in your place, as your substitute, so you do not have to go to hell. Jesus Christ is the only acceptable substitute for your sin.

"For He (God, the Father) made Him (Jesus) who knew (committed) no sin to be sin for us; that we might become the righteousness of God in him" (2 Cor. 5:21).

"I (Jesus) am the way, the truth, and the life. No one comes to the Father except through me" (Jn. 14:6).

"Nor is there salvation in any other, for there is no other name under heaven given among men by which we must be saved" (Acts 4:12).

Jesus Christ is your only hope and means of salvation. Because you are a sinner, you cannot pay for your sins, but Jesus paid the penalty for your sins by dying on the cross in your place. Friend, there is salvation in no one else – not angels, not some religious leader, not even your religious good works. No religious act such as baptism, confirmation or joining a church can save you. There is no other way, no other name who can save you. Only Jesus Christ can save you. You must be saved by accepting Jesus Christ's substitutionary sacrifice for your sins or you will be lost forever.

Do you see clearly that Jesus Christ is the only way to God in heaven? If you understand this truth, tell God that you understand and check the box below.

❏ *God, I understand that Jesus Christ died to pay the penalty for my sin. I understand that His death on the cross is the only acceptable sacrifice for my sins.*

4th Essential Spiritual Truth. <u>The Bible teaches that you must trust in Jesus Christ alone for eternal life and call upon Him to be your Savior and Lord</u>

Many religious people admit they have sinned. They believe Jesus Christ died for the sins of the world but they are not saved. Why? Thousands of moral, religious people have never completely placed their faith in Jesus Christ alone for eternal life. They think they must believe in Jesus Christ as a real person and do good works to earn their way to heaven. They are not trusting Jesus Christ alone. To be saved, you must trust in Jesus Christ alone for eternal life. Look at what the Bible teaches about trusting Jesus Christ alone for salvation.

> *"that if you confess with your mouth the Lord Jesus and believe in your heart that God has raised Him from the dead, <u>you will be saved</u>. For with the heart one believes unto righteousness, and with the mouth confession is made unto salvation . . . For there is no distinction between Jew or Greek, for the same Lord over all <u>is rich to all </u>who call upon Him. For <u>whoever calls on the name of the Lord shall be saved</u>" (Romans 10:9, 10, 12, 13).*

Do you understand what God is saying? To be saved or born again, you need to trust Jesus Christ <u>alone </u>for eternal life. Jesus Christ paid for your complete salvation. Jesus said, *"It is finished"* (John. 19:30). Jesus paid for your salvation completely when He shed His blood on the cross for your sin.

If you believe that God resurrected Jesus Christ, which proves God's acceptance of Jesus as a worthy sacrifice for man's sin, and you are willing to confess the Lord Jesus Christ as your Savior and Lord, master of your life, you will be saved.

Friend, right now God is offering you the greatest gift in the world. God wants to give you the <u>gift</u> of eternal life, the <u>gift </u>of His complete forgiveness for all your sins, and the <u>gift</u> of His unconditional acceptance into heaven when you die. Will you accept His free gift now, right where you are?

If you are unsure how to receive the gift of eternal life, review the essential spiritual truths:
1. You admitted you are a sinner.
2. You admitted your sin separates you from God you can't save yourself.
3. You realized that Christ is the only way to heaven – no other name can save you.
4. Now, you must call upon the Lord Jesus Christ to save your lost soul.

Ask Him right now to save you. Just take God at His word – He will not lie to you! This is the kind of simple faith you need to be saved. If you are still uncertain what to do, pray this prayer to God. Remember, the words must come from your heart.

> *God, I am a sinner and deserve to go to hell. Thank you, Jesus, for dying on the cross for me and for purchasing a place in heaven for me. Please forgive me for all my sins and take me to heaven when I die. I call on you, Jesus, right now to save me forever. Thank you for saving me now. Amen.*

If you just asked Jesus Christ to save you in the best way you know how, God just saved you. He said in His Holy Word, *"Whoever calls upon the name of the Lord shall be saved" (Romans 10:13)* and the **whoever** includes you – it's that simple. God just gave you the gift of eternal life by faith. You have just been born again according to the Bible.

You will not come into eternal judgment, and you will not perish in the lake of fire – you are saved forever! Read this verse over carefully and let it sink into your heart.

> **"Most assuredly, I say to you, he who hears My word and believes in Him who sent Me has everlasting, and shall not come into judgment, but has passed from death into life."** (John. 5:24)

Final Questions:
- According to God's Holy Word (John. 5:24), not your feelings, what kind of life did God just give you? _____ .
- What two words did God say at the beginning of the verse to assure you that He is not lying to you? _____ _____ .
- Are you going to come into judgment - <u>YES</u> or <u>NO</u>?
- Have you passed from spiritual death into life - <u>YES or NO</u>?

Friend, you have just been born again. You just became a child of God. We would like to help you grow in your new Christian life. We will send you a Spiritual Birth Certificate to remind you of your spiritual birthday and some Bible study materials to help you understand more about the Christian life. To receive these helpful materials free of charge, photocopy the form below, fill it out and send it to us by mail or e-mail us at resources @LamplightersUSA.org.

Lamplighters Response Card

Lamplighters International, 6301 Wayzata Blvd, St. Louis Park, MN, USA 55416

❑ I just accepted Jesus Christ as my Savior and Lord on (date) _____, 200____ at _____ .

❑ Please send me the Spiritual Birth Certificate and the Bible Study materials to help me grow as a Christian.

❑ I would like to begin attending a Bible-believing church in the area where I live. Please recommend some Bible-believing churches in the area where I live.

❑ I already know of a good Bible-believing church that I will be attending to help me grow as a new Christian.

Name _____

Address _____

City _____ State _____ Zip _____

Email address _____